BETWEEN THE THINNING DIFFERENCES OF CHANGING LIGHT

BETWEEN THE THINNING DIFFERENCES OF CHANGING LIGHT

New and Selected Poems

RICHARD D. FLOUT

Black Phoebe Press   San Rafael, California

Between the Thinning Differences of Changing Light
Copyright © 2025 by Richard D. Flout | Black Phoebe Press

Published in the United States November 2025
by Black Phoebe Press, San Rafael, California
For information, please contact the publisher: blackphoebepress@gmail.com

Grateful acknowledgment is made for permission to reprint previously printed material: "Let Your Colors Run," © 1979, and "The Thin Line of Light," © 1980, by Richard D. Flout, reprinted by permission of the *Blue Unicorn* poetry journal. "Remembering," © 1981, by Richard D. Flout, reprinted by permission of the *Suisun Valley Review*.

Cover art adapted from Joseph Mallord William Turner painting, "Norham Castle, Sunrise," © 1845, permission of the Tate Britain, London. Publisher's imprint adapted from artwork by Orxpikdesign / Dreamstime.com. Interior photographs: *pg. xv*, photosbyjim / iStock, Bowman Lake, Glacier National Park, Montana; *pg. 31*, Erik Eiser / iStock, Ventura, California; *pg. 55*, Lemanieh / iStock, Ruby Beach, Washington; *pg. 83*, JRP Studio / Shutterstock.

Library of Congress Control Number: 2025921986

Publisher's Cataloging-in-Publication
(Provided by Cassidy Cataloguing Services, Inc.)

Names: Flout, Richard D., 1950–author.

Title: Between the thinning differences of changing light : new and selected poems / Richard D. Flout.

Description: First edition. | San Rafael, California : Black Phoebe Press, [2025]

Identifiers: LCCN: 2025921986 | ISBN: 9798993410302 (paperback) | 9798993410319 (ebook) | 9798993410326 (downloadable audio file)

Subjects: LCSH: Poetry. | Poetic diaries. | Motivation (Psychology)—Poetry. | Inspiration—Poetry. | Nature—Poetry. | Hope—Poetry. | LCGFT: Poetry. | Autobiographies. | BISAC: POETRY / General. | POETRY / Subjects & Themes / General. | POETRY / Subjects & Themes / Motivational & Inspirational.

Classification: LCC: PS3606.L6828 B48 2025 | DDC: 811/.6—dc23

Book and cover design: Nola Burger www.nolaburger.com
Type: Whitman; Quasimoda

For the Presence within—
who aways guides, inspires, and loves,
no matter what.

*There is a floodtide of love washing toward you
and getting closer every moment.
So relax!
It's the end of us, you know—
death by gladness and wild connection.*

—RUMI

CONTENTS

Middle Years

Preface

Since my late teens and early twenties, poetry has been a spiritual companion that invites me to return to my deepest sense of self. It's like scripture to me. Poems can call one back to the most sacred, alive, and authentic parts of one's center. The path of poetry is a lifelong journey. I've put this book together to claim, honor, and share my journey with others.

In the mid-sixties, the lyrics of Bob Dylan's songs gave me permission to begin to ponder and make imaginative observations about family, relationships, the culture, and the world. Working as a landscape gardener in my twenties and thirties, poetry taught me to observe more acutely the natural world around me and to develop a more intimate relationship with it. Later, as a psychotherapist, I found by using powerful personal images and metaphors, my clients could get a deeper felt-sense of their truest identity. No matter what type of work or leadership I have done, poetry has been the lifeblood of any creative endeavor.

In 1979, it was my good fortune to begin seriously writing poetry while studying with Rosalie Moore, who had recently been nominated for the Pulitzer Prize for her book, *Year of the Children*. She helped me get two of my poems published in the *Blue Unicorn*, an internationally distributed poetry journal. A year later, I heard about a course being offered at UC Berkeley Extension titled, "Poems in Progress: A Workshop with Six American Poets," taught by Alan Soldofsky and guest teachers Margaret Atwood, Robert Bly, Gary Snyder, Caroline Kizer, and Philip Levine. On a whim, I decided to submit three poems, and, to my surprise, I was selected to attend out of a pool of 125 other Bay Area poets. One of my classmates, a young poet named Jane Hirshfield, soon drew the praise of Philip Levine, who, after reading one of her poems in class, remarked, "It's obvious this writer has a gift." Another night after class, the instructor came up to me. "The only reason that you got into this class," he said, "was because of one line of your submitted poems." That line, "between the thinning differences of changing light" from the poem, "Mystery of Edges," is the title of this book in honor of that bold decision by a young and budding poet to submit poems for a formative course.

May you enjoy this journey of poetry from the present day back to the beginning. As T. S. Eliot wrote:

"What we call the beginning is often an end.
And to make an end is to make a beginning.
The end is where we start from."

Richard D. Flout
November, 2025

NEW POEMS

2023–2025

The Movement I Become

The weeds and flowers
are here to accompany me
and the sun and moonlight
even the dark stars show
the path to move forward.
I can count on ocean waves
to keep me breathing,
the birdsong to open
my heart wider and longer.
What I know to be true,
the trunk of the oak tree
can bear my back
to give me rest.
The heavy rains and winds
clear my vision, bringing me
to surrender.
The constant turning of the seasons
teaches me how to change,
let go, and wait.
The early morning first light
and the quiet
falling of dusk
carry me.

An Early Glimpse

I remember that five-year-old boy
sitting next to a small fire
outside the large front door
of my father's auto repair shop,
where he had been burning boxes
of new parts bought to repair
his most recent job.

I found a 22-caliber bullet
lying in the gravel driveway
leading up to the garage.

Somehow, I knew it was wrong.
Somehow, I knew it was dangerous.

I felt comforted that my father
lay on the concrete floor
replacing a tailpipe and muffler
of an old Chevy truck
not so far away.

I held my breath,
tossed the bullet into the flames.
Nothing happened—then
a loud sudden crack.

I looked down at my arm
saw a three-inch line
of blood slowly emerge
where the blown off
copper casing ripped across
the skin of my forearm.

I waited for the worst,
but it turned out to be
a child's scratch.

In that moment
I met the possibility
of dying for the first time.
I knew then I was spared
to live another day,
with death now
a real and quiet
companion next to me.

I didn't tell my father.
I kept my secret
for myself.

Silence

You give me a space
to listen with ears
I cannot see.
You are a friend, always present;
we've been married for years.

Now, you introduce me
to my best thoughts and words.
You allow me to dwell with you;
at the same time, you are a companion
in and of your own.

I can return to you
at any moment, some say
nothing resembles God
more than you do.
You are a refuge
from loneliness and loss.

We got started together
under that giant pine
in the nursery grove
behind my childhood home.

I wish I could express
through grand poetry
what you mean to me,
but I know
you don't care about my words;
all I need to do
is to come, sit with you
and breathe.

A Cutting Edge Tool

It sits on my dresser
waiting days and months
to be useful,
clad in its regal red case
with its Swiss insignia.

What I love most:
those miniature scissors,
so small yet so facile.
You don't need to squeeze
both handles like the one
lying in my desk drawer;
you simply press on the outside
against a curved spring
and the scissor motion begins.

Such a delicate, elegant, fine cut
to paper, string, or a stray fiber
from a sweater or shirt,
easily and almost
secretly removed.

Ode to Rain

You keep falling, falling
water falls from the sky
reservoirs full to the brim,
some spilling over.
Luminescent green
grasses cover the hills.
Puddles everywhere.
Water rushes down gutters
alongside roads, draining
into culverts.

You teach us about flow,
about what it takes to be
alive and growing.
We would be dead
or dying without you.

You give us a lullaby
on the roof above our beds,
and with your companion, the wind,
you remind us how
powerless we truly are.

We can drink you,
wash ourselves clean
with you, as you sink
slowly into the earth,
touching deep roots and stones
earthworms and moles.

We are so alone without you.

You help us love the sun,
and when you two commune
in the sky, you gift us
with a bow of colors
in one long arch
across the meadows, our homes,
our streets, opening a gateway
to the hope of Moses,
freedom for all people.

Autumn Prayer

Red and yellow leaves
glow on thinning limbs, then fall
with the slightest breeze.
Everything basks in soft,
perfect light.

Buckeyes split
their leathery shells to reveal
bronze-colored faces.

Days shorten, darkness lengthens.

A time to give thanks
for plump figs and pumpkins
and prepare for a coming birth,
to drop deeper within, sit still,
and wait
for steady rain and hard wind
until the first green hints of spring
appear and hope of a new Earth
returns.

In the Strange Glare of the Sun

The photo sits on a bookcase
next to my bed.
My mother, in summer top and shorts,
shields her eyes
from the glare of the sun.
Her other hand holds onto mine.
This six-year-old boy,
dressed in a sports coat,
tie, and creased pants,
awkwardly looks down
and away, not wanting
to pose for the shot
being taken by my father,
in coveralls,
in front of his auto service shop.

(On the back of the photo,
my mother has written,
"I told my husband to hurry up,
for the sun was hurting my eyes,
and when I put my hand up to my face,
he snapped the picture.")

Recently, I showed the photo
to a friend. "You look
like a little man," he says.
I tell him
the little boy
lives in the woods
behind the shop. He sits
quietly beneath a tall
pine tree, his back
resting against its huge
and solid trunk.

How to Choose

It doesn't come from the outside,
even if it looks like it should.
Go inside, deep in your body,
listen for the voice
your blood and bones
tell you is true.

Discard all reasonable,
seductive thoughts.
It's going to come from
your lower belly, or in
a shadowy presence
almost on the other side
of who you know
yourself to be.

When you think you know,
pause a moment,
toss it up to the wind
to see if it takes flight
like a child's kite
climbing to the sun.

Even then, wait a little longer,
check for a glitch in your chest,
rigidity in your posture.
Say a prayer of consent.

Surrender to a sense
of deep love within
that doesn't care
whatever you happen to choose.
This love is not
about right or wrong;
only if it flows
like a spring stream
and rises like breath.

A Reconciliation

I hope I have served you well
so far, or at least of late.
I hope I have let
the wind chimes vibrate
long enough for their sounds
to soothe you when troubled.

I know I put you through some rough times:
not one, but two divorces,
not to mention all
the anxieties, guilts,
and insecurities that bound us
both to a wooden stake
in the ground.

You were probably wondering
when I would get it right,
when I would listen to where
you were whispering for me
to go.

I'm sorry.

I thought I was the emperor
of your field of flowers
with all my false alarms of
elevated blood pressure,
heart attack, irregular
heartbeat.

Now I know, you were trying
to show me which way to go.
I just couldn't believe
it could be easy
that I could relax,
relinquish the reins.

How could I have known?
I started from scratch.
No one seemed to see you
in those early days.

I hope I have served you well
today, as I will tomorrow.
I'm available as needed.

A Morning Prayer

A better morning.
A deep sleep cures all.

I gaze out a window
with a translucent
Japanese screen.

Alone with my page,
the heater hums
right next to me.

I see an old oak
glistening with new rain.
A small yellow leaf
twirls to the ground.

I don't know how long
I will be here.
I don't know where
I will go.

Can such mystery
release me
from thinking too much
or too long
about now.

Opening to Love

Once, while scrambling
through the underbrush on Mt Baldy,
I heard a slight
rustle in the bushes
and quickly lifted my field glasses.
In the frame of the lenses,
a hermit thrush
quietly perched,
dark-eyed, staring back at me.
An unexpected moment,
an intimacy, eye to eye.
Each of us
discovering the other
in silent stillness,
a communion of presence
in the early morning.

Lost in Prayer

Merton says
breathing is prayer.
I think I agree.

One sits or stands
or walks along a street
and breathes,
without knowing
where the breath
comes from, or where
it goes.

I close
my eyes, sit
in silence
in a room or backyard.
Who knows where
the prayer begins
and where it ends.
Does it end or begin
at all. Is prayer
about being alive
right now, all the time?

Who are you, prayer?
A state of mind,
a moment of being,
a relationship with an Other,
unseen and sacred;
held deeply
in the skin of my heart,
the hairs of my head?

Prayer,
are you music,
or are you laughter?

You are elusive,
of mystery,
a secret embrace
in the moonlight
in the darkness
before morning.

The Next Step

After the last word falls
and the first foot rises
to take the next step,
the world opens
into a vast darkness—
with light at its center.

So many people walk
next to each other,
looking to see where
the path may go.
This is no help, nor
the way to know
the road each of us
must go.

Go where we feel
most alive.
Let this place vibrate
like a tuning fork
seeking notes
of resonance,
or an acapella choir
melding harmonies
into a single voice.

Who knows
where this harmony resides,
in the trees, or inside
a chamber of the human heart?
Perhaps, in the chorus of crickets
as night slips into a hidden light.

We can move forward
with the instinct of animals
move toward
the unravelling of all
fixed and certain
notions of who we are.

After the last word
falls and the first foot
steps into the unknown
we have not seen
or hoped for.

After the last word
falls, and the first breath
taken without thought,
a secret spirit
moves toward running waters,
a setting sun.

A River's Lament

The river sings a sadness
of love.
Deep waters, dark
blue and green,
rush toward rocks
and fall
into a canyon
below.

Why does the river sing
of a sadness?

It has known the joy
of carrying a swimmer's body,
a wooden vessel to the mouth
of a sea.

A lifeline to the explorer
of caves and inlet bays.

A watery burial ground
for pelicans, grebes, sea otters
and seals.

Blackened, covered, and coated
with crude spills,

no longer able to fly
float or breathe.

The river sings a sadness—

for the turtles, dolphins and whales
suffocated by mountains
of plastic on ocean floors.

The river sings a sadness—

while sunlit lovers lie
cuddled, asleep on the shore.

Hope

pieces
       of a dream ...
soft, gray
       shadows
of eucalyptus
       leaves
dance on
       a white wall.
early,
       this strange
morning,
       I see
a hidden
       door
it is
       open.

Crossing Over Route 18

1. I remember when I was four years old
holding my breath,
crossing over Route 18,
the busiest and only highway
in the Western Pennsylvania town
I grew up in,
to be with my much older
brother, who worked at the Texaco
on the other side.

When I returned
hand in hand with my brother,
like a reluctant prodigal son,
my mother came up
with the well-intentioned idea
of putting me in a playpen
in our backyard.

She asked my father,
a master craftsman,
to build one—so he did.
The moment I heard
the latch on the gate
snap shut, crated like a pup,
I vowed to
spend all my time
getting out.

I got down on my hands and knees
like a one-year-old labrador
pawing at the earth
in a forbidden
garden bed.   >

I must have dug for hours.
By afternoon, a space
large enough now
between the gate's bottom
and the ground.
I slipped my small body
underneath like a thread
passing through the eye
of a needle.

When my mother spotted me
running around behind our house,
her face a mix of anger
and terror, she called my father,
who left his shop to come
to the scene of my escape.
He said, "It's obvious he doesn't
want to be in this thing."

He tore it down the next day
like a Tibetan Buddhist monk
wiping away a mandala
drawn in sand.

II.   Now, I've driven a 1966
Volkswagen beetle
loaded down
like a three-quarter-ton pickup truck
across the Great Plains
over the Rockies in dark
blinding thunderstorms
with multiple breakdowns,
to go to graduate school
in Northern California.

I've run the gauntlet
of 3000 hours of face-to-face
training, a written and oral
exam in a hotel room
to get a counselor's license,
among other interns
quivering with anxiety.

I have survived
the horror and shame
of two divorces.
But nothing, nothing
compares to the moment
my head poked through that opening
into the spacious air,
a holy call, ever since
for a life to come.

Last Days at Santa Sabina

Through the cross
of the windowpanes
of an upstairs retreat room
at Santa Sabina,
I take in
the white bark
of a birch,
its yellow leaves
shaped like tiny hearts.

A red sweetgum
set aflame by autumn
afternoon sunlight
rises high above
wooden benches and
picnic tables, little spots
to sit and be.

How many times
how many people,
myself included
(nearly fifty years),
welcomed
into this heavenly realm.

Will it still go on
after the doors close,
the chapel taken down.
Will new visitors
take the time to breathe in
the stillness of the grounds below?

Today, like every day
here, a sacred refuge
to gather,
to sigh and pray,
resting
in solitude and quiet
in a room, sitting
by a window.

Getting My Bearings

I am lost today.
A branch fallen to the ground.

Yet, the white-crowned sparrow
touches down on a distant limb,
his diamond jewel flashes in the breeze.

The pyracantha's snowy early blossoms
add a coolness to this spring afternoon.

A squirrel dashes along the top edge
of the deck fence behind my house.

He is always earnest
in every movement, as he disrespectfully
digs in the soil beneath a 75-year-old
bonsai tree.

Hummingbirds buzz in and out
of the feeder, elevating
like miniature helicopters,
after a quick taste of sweetness.

What can I say, the living
go on living, the dead
only wait for the next moment.

Then, there is the vulture,
a winged lover of death
wobbling in the air,
balancing itself on the wind.

Once, a wake of vultures with precise intent,
cleansed the corpse of a day-old fawn
fallen in the backyard,
turning it into a matted patch of green
in a matter of hours.

I was lost today.
Now out my window,
a white-tailed raptor stills
above a single spot
in the field below.

New Identity

I have no signature anymore.
It's illegible,
morphed into a pile
of swirling lines,
an autograph one needs
to peer into deeply
to find a person.

My name became too small
and burdensome to bother with.

Now, no one
will recognize me—
known, only as memory,
a shimmering
in a flickering presence.

LATER YEARS

2005–2023

Healing Chant

When I have no peace
I lie down in the darkness.

When I have no purpose
I stare long at a tree.

When I have no meaning
I jump into the moment.

When I have no company
I sleep with the birds.

When I have no friends
I remember my mother.

When I have no mother
I walk in the woods.

When I have no patience
I cry into my hat.

When I have no music
I reach for a hand.

When I have no time
I sit down and wait.

Unspoken Eulogy for Philomena

Mother, you tracked me like a hound,
measured my every step,
but you did know what I could do
and even if you were hell-bent on
getting me to do what you wanted,
you taught me to love nature as a friend
as you did your peonies in the backyard.

You taught me my first prayer
knowing that I had a relationship with God
ready for the asking.
You sat me down to watch Laurel and Hardy,
the Marx Brothers, declaring: "This is good comedy."

Underneath you were mad or at least sad
when I left town; I know you wanted me to have
a richer, fuller life than you.

I knew this when
you sent me the article
about the priest
who gave the two boys an old Cadillac
so they could drive to California.

I knew this was your way
of saying you were glad
I made my own life.

After your death, the family was surprised
to find your hidden drawings
tucked away in your paperback novels
stacked on the stand by your reading chair.
You were hard to talk to—and even harder
to get to listen, but I want to thank you
for who you were.
I'm sorry you and I didn't get to know
the person
you really were.

A Dark Jaguar

Paces in a cage of bones,
eyes widen, teeth glistening,
dying to cry out
a primal sound of origin,
where the sun
moon and earth align
in the early morning.

Full of explosive, lush
energy, the jaguar longs
to release
animal soul within.

The jaguar, a bridge
to the heavens, where
all music, poetry,
and art flow downward,
deeply penetrating the body
of the earth below.

Where does all this energy go…
What can it become?

I sit quietly in its presence
hope for angels
prayers and scriptures
to guide me through
this fertile time.

Unaware of such force
within, I am stunned
into a river of laughter,
cries of loss, and the joy
of new arrivals
throughout my body
and bones.

Listen to the dark jaguar.
Look into the black stars.
Fall endlessly into realms
of humility, praise,
and wild grace.

Ants

We love community…

We gather
in small hills.

We love
to push and shove
tiny bits of earth
all day long.

We never stop…

We dig tunnels,
our colonies
deep in the ground.

Loyal servants
to our hidden
subterranean queen,
we deliver particles
of food
while she lays
and tends to eggs.

Not many know
she exists—
unless they dig deep
to discover
our secret farm,
our persevering
underground culture.

We will be here
in our basement civilization,
along with the cicadas,
long after
all larger life
has disappeared
from our forgotten Earth.

What Did I Know

It was my first visit.
Never spoke to a therapist.
In my mind, didn't need it.
What was this upper class
old woman from Belvedere
with her hair tied up in a bun
going to teach me.

Near the end of the session
she asked, "What are you
afraid of most?"

"To fail," I told her.

She responded,
"It's been my experience that people
who are afraid to fail
are supposed to."

Her words startled
and shook me.
I heard her say something
I had never thought of before.
I knew then, I was not alone,
and hung on her every word
till the day she died.

The Island of Poetry

Always discovered
as a new place, where
harmonies and rhythms play and sing.
Emptying souls meet here daily,
share acute observations.
Monks, street musicians, and prophets
congregate under palm trees.
Here, they taste papayas and mangoes,
listen for the cries of macaws
echoing under the canopy of rainforest,
breathing in the moisture
dripping from the tips of giant ferns
high in the crooks of trees.

Someone and Something Revealed

FOR BOB DYLAN

Right before that sudden,
opening snap
of the snare drum
woke me out of an afternoon
daydream walking the aisles
of Hall's department store.

You began singing,
"Once upon a time,"
just like a child's nursery
rhyme, then went on to
shout out,
"How does it feel?"

Not once, but twice—
"How does it feel
to be without a home
like a complete unknown."

Now my sixteen-year-old heart,
pierced by such strange new words,
hears—for the first time—
someone describe how
I felt inside
but didn't know it.

All the solitary grief
hidden under the floorboards
of the old homestead.

"How does it feel?'

No one ever asked
me that so fiercely
so directly.

Thank you for your inquiring voice,
an unlikely prophet
pointing out the ignored obvious.

Till this day,
when I hear
your awakening call
your insistent refrain,
my heart swells
my bones rumble
tears begin to rim my eyes.
I'm "invisible now."
I've "got no secrets to conceal."
"How does it feel?"
"How does it feel?"

Receive and See

Red pyracantha berries glow
in the morning sun. Eucalyptus
leaves dangle like soft green
knife blades outside my window.
To live in two realms of time,
to witness shootings, murder,
and war.

To receive love, a transforming
moment, solid stone into
flowing water, a river carries
us away beyond what's
alive or dead
to the next moment where love
resides, deep
in the center of each person.

How can each realm together be?
We suffer for the chance to change,
to rearrange our past into
a new present, where
kindness, mercy, and grace lead us
back to the morning garden,
daffodil bulbs emerging, azaleas bursting
in a new view
from a new window.

Unknown Sanctuary

Death informs us
of the spirit in one's life.
Listen to the wind
watch the movement
of waves. Everything alive
moves between birth
and death, death and birth.
How we make the journey,
what guides our souls,
appears at the time
of any death.

There is nothing in the world
to hold on to.
Little by little we let go
of each piece
of that daytime dream,
until we find ourselves
resting inside
a body of grace.

When we touch into the unknown
allowing it to become a sanctuary—
even if only within
your own silence,
you may know now
how to stand in this world.

Spiral of Life

Naked surrender gives each of us
a true home next to water.
Our uniqueness carries us into
community with the whole.

Mary, a crowned frog, and deep tree
roots bring each of us
to the presence of the woman
with the owl, rendering our hearts
open with gratitude and praise.

Swirls of sand, small pools of water
take us into the holy
presence forever in us
coming to us.

Mid-Afternoon Meditation

Quiet afternoon in a room,
a large window faces
sky, clouds, trees,
and red roofs.
Weary, perhaps bored
and lost somewhat
on a page.
This is the place to
begin, to start from here
and move toward freedom,
elusive yet nearby.
What is there to pursue
today, but this moment
sitting still, listening
to the silent buzz
distant cars
swish down the road.
A doe lies beneath
an old oak tree, looks out
over the hillside.
Can this be enough
to fall into?
I want to fall
into the deep
silence and breathe.

Bringing Milk Through Snow

Won't you walk with me
to the next junction...
What I lost maybe
you can help me find.

Born during the deepest snowfall,
my father struggled through drifts
to feed me.

Here I stand an old man,
wondering where I will go tomorrow.

My one eye looks out,
my other eye looks within.
Something has arrived,
deep in my heart.

The Surprise of Age

The surprise of age,
how it haunts in each day
after sixty. A new pain each year,
some last a short while, others for
months to nearly a year.

Eyesight lessens, memory fades
one moment to the next.
And hearing, you miss a word or two,
filling in your own imagined
conversation with friends, clients or
while watching movies.

But with age, no longer any need
for mastery to prove worth. One can
simply receive, sing
acapella, write a poem,
play the ukulele. One can
linger in the arms of love longer,
with little need for more than
simple tender intimacies.

No need to be somebody.
You know,
deep down to the soles of your feet,
the sweetest truth of all…
not what I am but
that I am—right here,
now.

Only Child

When I become world-weary,
I sit down under a tall northern pine
and listen to the wind
blowing through the limbs above me.

I listen more closely
for the stillness of the soil,
the emptiness of the nursery woods.

I stop my mind from traveling,
touch my hand to the earth.
I know who I am
and where I belong.

The world larger now,
for a moment
I can rest
in the silent spaces
between the trees.

Meeting the Day

Pull on my work boots,
go out the front door.
Take a look for what's green,
growing, or what's languid
on the stem.

Snip off anything extra
or intrusive of other plants.
Pause a moment,
to savor all in bloom.
Put my hands in the soil
separate weeds from seedlings.

Make sure of harmony
in placing pots of geranium.
Pick off a dead bloom
or small branch, expose the vibrant
yellows and reds.
Stop. Sit on the bench.
Listen to the silent
flutter, the buzz
the secret calls and songs.

When It Gets Warm Things Slow Down

A turkey vulture swoops
then glides over the sun
bleached hills. A gentler
breeze jostles the tips of pine,
an occasional car
echoes as it moves
behind oaks and hills.

Summer day in August
heat and air mix
to make this afternoon
a soul time, a restful time,
subtle movements, distant voices
a note or two of birdsong.

Here I am, in time
and out of time,
listening, looking,
this summer afternoon
waiting for nothing
hoping for nothing.
Is there anything
I could want but
this moment now.

Grace Awaits

I am made real living simply
to rise early, wash my face,
trim my beard. Enjoy oatmeal.
Just give me a window—beyond
sky, clouds, hills, and trees.
A monk at heart, content
to sit in a room.
I bathe my body with silence,
where there is nothing I must do
to know love.

MIDDLE YEARS

1985–2005

Closer to the Bay

It hasn't been long now
since the cable snapped
and the rain stopped.
The oak exposes its roots,
its trunk leans a little closer to
the bay. I grab my rake, take up
the wind-shook leaves. I pause
before Spring, invite the buds
to resist the continuous rain.
I sharpen my shears for the days
when sun and moisture
mingle, and I am
no longer in control
of this green light
within and all around.

When Night Is Welcome

We struggle so much with the surface
of things, while our hearts remain
caged, herded like children
into rooms.
We hope for appearances,
to take us home,
but there is no comfort here,
for we do not know what we want,
our longing converted
into tickets for the show,
held out, torn, and left with the stub
to get in and get out.

In the dark all the night is ours,
not just a colored screen
that hangs from a ceiling
in front of a row of chairs,
but the whole well of night,
into the mystery of nature,
woman and man, we merge.
There, in our own incompleteness,
we are found by a shared
breath, the gift of each of us
unique, not to be taken away.
And we cry out,
"Help me in my darkness."

The night grows wide,
a bird flies from hidden limbs
and the moon,
no longer an omen,
lays its light at our feet
where we walk as in snow,
owning each footprint
pressed firmly into the white
of night.

Nightfall

Occasional footsteps
(people in the next apartment)
make solitude loud in a large empty room.
Sound enters the body
and takes on its mood.

Shoes without feet
and legs thrown off
clutter the floor.
Alone, a sickle-shaped moon
climbs the silhouette of a fir tree.
Night is a constant
companion, even by day,
clinging to the spaces between bones.

All my windows are black,
reflecting in them the back wall
of my room. Like a fantasy
or dream, I see the doorway,
the closet full of clothes,
photos on the wall.
All the light around me glows
mysterious, without direction.
As the crickets insist
on night.

A Gardener's Rainy Day

it rains.
across the haze of my eyes
behind a windowpane.
the drops crackle
as they hit, awakening
a face too small
to smile at the way
it tightens the time,
without work or plan.

it rains.
across the glass of my room
the drops slide
as they break flat,
not touching the hour.
I lie on a couch,
one leg resting its length,
the other bent at the knee,
foot pressed flat against the floor,
ready to rise, move,
and prune.

Arguing with Choice

Simply say yes or no.
The rest comes from the doubt
that robs us of who we are.

Do not be tricked into thinking
you have no choice,
condemned to live
between your longings
and self-made laws.

Spirit needs no explanations.
You are talking to the past,
to voices introduced
into your blood like venom.

Simply say yes or no.
This is enough to know.
Move in your yes.
Stand in your no.

A tree does not argue with the rain,
nor the river bicker with the stones.
It's music, the yes of all nature.

Come, listen
to the deer cracking the brush.
Come, listen
to the sparrows sing
their sure notes.

Simply say yes or no.
Find yourself in the center of justice,
form your lips, feel the words…
our life depends on
yes and no.

Are you finished now?
Then believe it and go.

Anticipating Spring

This is late winter,
a moment of pause in nature;
a still moment,
when life aches for witness.

Bulbs cleave the earth,
my eyesight revives.
How many times
can this be the *first* time,
I wonder.

But spring seems too much
to ask. Even though today
has a different sun, a slow
yet steady heat warming
the back of my neck,
sweat remembered.

Should I dare uncover
my skin, my summer's watch?
This is late winter,
a moment of pause
when the ground moves
for an instant.

The Witness

He is here now, the man with the lonely feet.
He says his heart no longer fits him.
He cries as he sings.
I thought I would never meet him,
the man with the lonely word.
He says he has always been here,
waiting for one eye to open
and the spell lifted by new air.

I get scared when he stands here
alone, ready to change.
He says, "you're too small
to breathe the way animals do."
I ask him not to go again.
He says he has always been here;
he breathes, as he breaks.

Spring Begins

A crow caws in the ravine
below as I rest eye level
with wild hyacinth, purple
sanicle, and cranesbill.
They grow up in
the spaces of an old
and fallen oak limb.
Grass stands erect
among the flight of the fresh
new flies of spring.
Buttercups open, gather in,
and reflect the immense
yellow of the sun.
Winter remembered
in the moss,
still bright green on the oak branch.
The sound of creek water
moves within still-time
flowing long after jet engines
have torn the sky.
In the distance
I can hear human voices
rising up
out of a thicket of trees.

Instead of Love

FOR PHILIP LEVINE

A climbing rose grows up the outhouse.
Willow, the camp dog, takes a crap
in mounds of freshly cut grass.
He is content
to sniff behind beams,
to wag a stubby tail,
each day is a day to live
in whatever way suits him.
Green branches bend like a bow
over the wooden deck
where he sits.

More than Memory

An old man sits on a bench
in the San Anselmo town park,
his left hand cupped over his left knee.
He takes an occasional puff
from a cigar and simply watches.
A black Great Dane dashes across the grass.
The old man bows his head, looks down
to the sidewalk as if hoping to see something
he has never seen before.
He flicks an ash, checks his watch,
a Spanish nanny walks by with a little girl
and says hello. Nods his head,
lets out a big puff of smoke,
then examines the inside edge
of his right shoe.
He watches a young girl play with her dog,
follows them with his eyes
until they walk out of view.
He gets up
and walks slowly down the sidewalk
between the leaf-scattered lawn.

The Playground

A football flies through the air,
screams and shouts, explosions of energy
school children hold.
Two boys slap at each other,
wrestling with arms entangled.
Little Catholic girls in uniform skirts
bounce a basketball on asphalt
marked off with white lines.

> two inland gulls fly over
> as if the Pacific is below

Motion within motion.
A boy crashes to the pavement
and names hollered:
"Tina! Tina! Here!"

> a newspaper flaps against a gate
> of a cyclone fence

"The ball! The ball!"

Approaching Autumn

Summer is surely gone now.
I can tell by the shivering
in my chest, and by all the yellow
leaves, drooping like flags
without wind.
I look down at the ground,
worn to a finish by trampling
of active summer feet.

I feel alone, like the patches
without grass.

The iris brown shoot still hangs
in the air, a shadow now
of the flower it used to be,
its long leaves lie scattered
and look like a place
dogs have played.

I was eight years old
when Sid and me
would crawl on our bellies
like invading marines
to the old man's yard at the end of our street.
He grew grapes. We knew if we could
sneak up on the side of the arbor that faced
away from his back window, we could
sit and feast with the arbor itself as our screen.

When we got there
we squeezed the centers into our mouths
threw away the skins, leaving a pile
as a monument to our fill.

That was twenty-seven years ago,
and I am approaching autumn again.

Today

I want to steal some grapes.

A Birthday Poem

Born in November,
when changing leaves outdo spring colors,
when the movement of death becomes
more radiant than birth, in this time of
going inward and losing all
that's simply attached.
To know a love will not be created
with the right recitation of words
or the most passionate of dream-thoughts,
that it all comes down to sitting still,
watching the leaves fall
when the mornings turn cold.

Born in November,
I have finally come to love
this thanksgiving time, this pilgrim time,
touching the bare trunk, seeing
thinning limbs not as a threat
or sign of loss, but to know this empty time—
this empty body—is the home of my peace.

Born in November,
this season of coming to know
what's left when the green
of the ginkgo tree
empties itself into many fans
of golden light.

The Buddha

He sits.

One hand raised as if to touch,
The other rests on his thigh,
Palm up, receiving all he has not.
His brow, solid and sure,
Eyes almost closed,
Open enough to know

He sits.

His robe falls over his body
Like water over a rock,
Knees bent flat
Form a base, teaching how

He sits.

His mouth is sealed, serious
Yet almost smiling.
Each ear has grown larger than most.
He hears a sound
Deep inside the Earth where

He sits.

A Robbery

Pruning in a garden
at work, a flash of orange
flies overhead. I look up,
excited, hoping to spot
a rare California bird.
It's a blue jay,
boldly clamped in its bill
a plank of cheddar cheese
taken from my lunch sack
that sat inside the open
window of my truck.

The Mailbox

This blue bin
holding checks, letters, and junk
stands bolted to a cement slab.
A steel box where people drop off
many messages, pay off
many debts.

This blue bin
a receptacle for all
words written down, printed, and colored,
transferring a message from one
narrow opening
to another.

Elegy for an Estranged Son

A wincing young man's face
the talk of his parent's separation
brought up to his ears,
a shuffle of feet,
a quick smile, inappropriate,
it does not work here.

He says, "I don't have a lot to say to him."
Concerned, he plans to spend the fall
living with him
while going to school.
"Perhaps a time of healing," I suggest.
He says, "Let's not hear any more
talk about healing."

I suspect he will spend his nights
alone in his room
studying his books, studying
the walls, protecting
so nothing gets disturbed,
but the air is easily contaminated
by secrecy and sidesteps.

Let's hope for a sudden burst of
sorrow, or a small tear
in the bathroom early some morning
when the mirror is clear
as he stares beyond the spots
of toothpaste on the glass,
surprised to see,
his father in the doorway,
ready to ask a question.

The Return

It is important to give yourself
a whole day by the ocean
in the sand to allow your belly
to slowly fill with the joy
and sorrow long held up
somewhere in your chest.
As my eyes look into your eyes
it is there again, the tenderness
that exists between a hollow stomach
and eyes edging up to tears.
I never thought I would ever witness
such love as this moment now.

It is hard to bear
more than a few minutes of such
tender spirit, such vibration
of skin and bone.
I've been dead a lot
longer than I have known…
I've been a lover
of the dead, the futile
and the disowned.

And so now, as I breathe in
the new air freshened by ocean
mist, I allow it to pass
deeply into the bottom
of this once abandoned
body, slowly being furnished
again, to home
a whole person.

Morning Renewal

Shall I listen to the sunlight
sermon offered to me
each morning when I awake,
or will I dig my own
solitary tunnel
to preserve my image of surety?

Today, I choose to listen
to the ladies of the land
and allow them to walk me
slowly back to my soul.
I shall kneel down
next to the deep well,
the fertile ground,
and draw up slowly
my taste of the freshest
spring water.

Then, the love on my lips
will be revealed
in the faces of strangers and friends,
and I shall walk this day
upright, whole and alive,
giving thanks
to the moon, the roses,
and a bird
returning to its perch.

On Silent Retreat

As the light dims and the greens
become darker, I wait
for no one, for no thought.
If waiting is necessary at all,
I wait to sleep,
to dream of the foggy light
the morning to come and all its
possibilities.
A woman draws water for her horses,
only ninety feet away.
I could call to her,
start a conversation, but I'm here,
a part of only the mist and fog
slowly taking over
the last outline of trees.

Peace at the End of Tomales Point Trail

A time so calm, no wind.
A clear sky above the ocean.
I rest my head among seaside daisies.
Red ants roam the terrain of their vast world,
bumble bees carry yellow bundles
from one open flower to another.
A squadron of pelicans
glides through the air like jets
in formation before their comical,
awkward plunge for fish.
There is nothing I want to become.
Nobody and nothing I want to change.
Alone, but not alone
by the sea.

Empty Pitcher

Now is the time
Not to know anything
Not to hold on to anything
To listen to the birds sing
To watch the buds open
And know something
Is coming toward you
Something you can't earn
Something you can't steer
A promise you were born
To reveal and live
There is no answer
Only an experience
Of more life ahead
Only an empty pitcher
Being filled
With the freshest water

A Beautiful Garden

O living breath
That stirs inside me like wind
In a storm
How I love to be blown by You
How free and wild I feel
A child running through the fields.
This I know
You are here now
With me
Breathing in that wind
Breathing in my soul
I'm so happy
You are here
Violet violas
Yellow marigolds
Such a beautiful garden
Inside my heart.

EARLY YEARS

1975–1985

The Ring of Keys

Old keys and locks,
Metal and holes,
Too many
Ideas that close.
I lost a key once,
Have you?
Fifteen keys to own just one.
Only one.
Diamonds and bracelets,
Too many stones,
Only one
Is enough.

The Sun Gets in My Way

Motionless I see,
catching the cause
upon the shimmering grass...
Time, I hear you,
breaking in the breeze.

Motionless, I move
with waves of green hair
breathing beyond silence;
the sun gets in my way
deeply,
sparkling the surface
of my eyes.

Mystical Opening

I wish I could move along
the waters,
sliding like mercury
on a mirror.

I push through the wind
catching glints of light.
How can I move with the flow
of the mirrored waters?
How can I stay
within the stream of breathing?

I slide slowly yet steadily
holding the wind,
guarding my eyes from stars
of water
flickering the sun.

Above the bending darkness
mountains stand firm
watching over lapping water
from summits of light.
I fall to my knees.

In my first yielding,
I receive
the water's silver.

Mystery of Edges

I. Hidden in the glass of midnight
there is a silence—
a silence that slows
the twenty horses,
running headlong.

II. The birds beg for the morning
not of women nibbling
on apple cores for breakfast,
or men leaning
on hollow pencils for nothing,
but for the native morning
sprayed with the mist of sunlight
laced with the speckled blur
of woodpecker wings.

III. I am a native hunter now;
arched like a crow,
cracking the bark of seeds,
waiting for the spawning salmon
to fly like silver spears
through the opening of dawn.

IV. It's time, it's time today
to fish by hand,
skimming stones for scales
while gripping the bank
of the widening edge
between the thinning differences
of changing light.

How Near Is the Foreign Country?

Here, we are
collected in a living room,
piecing together videotape,
rumors, and newspaper headlines,
our hearts held hostage
by ideology and camera shots
of various political parades.

We talk truth.
We talk right and wrong.
We talk the evening into thoughts,
only a murmuring of unrest.

It is not in the assassination, but inside
this single minute at home.
Where is the struggle?
So easily we step around,
turning away from an infant grandmother,
a slow son, a crying man.
Is our conflict in Afghanistan
or Iran?
We honor ourselves by struggling with countries.

Each of us speaks through distant slumber,
tears turned under.
Here we build our defense,
political maneuver, nuclear warhead.
Here, inside
in this single minute
where a muted child is
unheard by closest ears.

In a Drought Year

NORTHERN CALIFORNIA, 1977

I. Winter comes unwashed
and warm, weary for rain.
The rain falls in drizzles,
blackened clouds betray
the hardened earth
that bears
a tearless pain.

II. Shallow-rooted
camellias burn with sunlit heat,
yellow in the chafing wind.
Pyracantha Christmas berries
hang like brown-rotting apples,
while a drying wind blows
spores of fire blight
to infect
a sapless spring.

III. Spring creeps slowly, instinctively,
like delusion preying on zealous minds.
Upon this gentle green
aphids stick
to bulge their bodies,
sucking and draining
the last droplets of sap
like loveless men who milk
a dry cow, a memory for love.

Even the steel cords of ivy,
cemented and newly wound,
succumb to the silver slime
tracked by snails
huddled,
on dusty ground.

IV.   Yet, among all this,
spring bursts through the iron haze
to show herself
in conspicuous red roses
that pucker and pose,
then droop,
wrinkled
on arid wind.

V.   I can't remember days as dry as these,
bringing me to the parched spot
where God is lost
along the cracks
of chapped creek beds,
and a lone rock rose
awaits the flare of summer's
impending sun.

With Eyes Set on Jerusalem

I.   With eyes
set on Jerusalem
I relive the tribes
I visit new villages.
Lost in the smoke of deserts
I walk a road, darkened
by the hooves of animals roaming
below the trees, circling
the tracks of men's sandals.

II.   The feet of men, the broken
tools, they cross
sloping sands with sun
twisted faces,
slipping in tracks too deep
to be recalled.

III.   I huddle in a haze
knees against my chest
thinking of Jesus
my scarf across my lips.

IV.   His words, unheard,
fall on the skin
of ears, deadened
by the calling for fires
to burn
their needed enemies.

V. It's hard to give up
    grumblings
    and questionings—sometimes
    the only distance between
    a sand-sprayed past
    and the open palm.

VI. In the stillness of dawn,
     I rise to see
     yet another village.
     With eyes set
     on Jerusalem,
     I go.

Good Friday, 1978

I am brow-weary.
The breast of branches nailed.
Clearly there is no question.
The palm and its green veins
tighten the toil of silence,
a silence that stops
at nothing, until it stops.

Fingers drag along a margin
between the old rags of skin
and the open star of Death,
whose blood-beating heart jars
our fever and bones.
Too many times we are tricked
into shells,
into flesh-hard nails of reasons.

A holy invitation is tonight.
When ribs are squeezed to powder
and a son receives his father;
closing his eyes
inside the barking dark closet,
he can hear the heat of Hands
rubbing off the smears
of charcoal roses.

Another October Dream

In the shifting autumn air,
the bones begin to break,
a dying limb on an infant tree.
What can be lonelier than death of self?
I need a leaf to still these fragile bones.

I see my mother's face in the evening fog,
I shield my eyes from my father's caring eye.
A child whimpers to the wind.

I sweat in time with silent cramps of doubt,
my feet blistered raw
for having traveled so far.

Who knows how to breathe with the birds,
pray like the squirrels, die like the worms?
Shake wind, shake loose my sapless skin,
and form footprints on the leaf-laden ground.
For the night, like a knife, nudges my soul forward.
How many deaths can one life hold?

In that first light,
when the hills begin to gather in the fog,
I can hear the gardener
raking up the dead.

At the Tip of Baja: The First Days of Marriage (1979)

I. Where the Sea of Cortez
    and the Pacific meet,
    the waves explode like cannons,
    splattering white sound all along the shore.

    We sit on a porch
    feet propped on wrought iron
    watching for a star to flash.
    At night the sand glows
    like a well-trodden snowfield
    as the shore waits
    for the white hands
    of a wild sea.

    You go on to bed
    (no star flash tonight)
    and I remain outside
    in envy of this sea
    with thunder in its breath.

II. Everything is different
    in a strange country: trees
    are like bushes full of flowers,
    crabs live in holes
    and are white.

    On the sand a crab pauses
    alone, waiting to move…
    ahead only horizon, mist
    separating sky from sea.

I am away from home—
not even the Coca-Cola cans
will console my distance.
Marriage is a long idea
to embody, each individual
breath coming together
slowly, in a room
air-conditioned, where words are
foreign, and not enough.

III.   Sitting in the shadow
of a great stone
with graffiti tattooed on its back,
I watch the suds of this sea
constant as breath,
sliding and rolling along the shore,
leaping in the air like rows
of dolphins.

The mountains become
statues of ancient chiefs
petrified by the spirit of the sea,
permanent as great men.

IV.   Freedom lies deep
in a leaping wave
foaming water
in the draw of undertow.
I fear the downward pull,
its tilting, sliding floor, at once
everything changing.   >

It makes me light-headed
standing inside
this pull, watching the million
raindrops run down the sand
back to the sea,
erasing crab tracks, footholds,
and age.

First Words of a Child

To know what words to speak,
worn like a glove
on the tongue,
protecting the palate
from the sting of snow
or the heat of a mouth.

The words of a child
afraid to talk—
of father leaving
or mother dying—
crawling on hands
and knees
across the trestle,
afraid of falling
through the spaces
between the tracks,
not speaking
his words.

Those words
squeezing their way
through the pupils
of his heart,
opening a lip
with tear-soft fingertips
of sound.

I hear your words
breathing in my ears,
but the child knows now
what words to speak...
I need.
I want.

Love Comes Forth with Every Death

A SONNET FOR VERA

What lies behind the sealed eyes of men
Whose bodies now, remain no more than stone?
I pray that I might see my love again
Without the human hold of blood and bone.
Does the star turn black to join the night
As primrose crushed, submits beneath the boot;
Or does it shine with brighter beams of light
Because the bud has not become the fruit?
Although I chill within the shadows cast
Upon the place that mortal clouds conceal,
The sooty shades of gray retreat at last,
As eyes of love begin to break the seal.
And I will know the star and rose are one
When I behold the moon eclipse the sun.

Boyhood

When I reach the wind,
my head shrinks and I come alive.
I see the branches,
graphing the sky.

I scribble my name in mud,
look through bubbles
of hot tar
on the pavement of my grade school days...
the asphalt ramp, rubber-stained
by the friction of boys.
I see the brick schoolhouse
that looked like the Alamo,
the loft, the plaza,
the parking lot,
Grant's garden shop;
and all the hallways
I trampled through
fields of goldenrods
as tall as my father.

I drift along tadpole gutters
and hide among high weeds,
waiting for
grasshoppers to tick.
I dash across long fields,
my feet digging in like hooves,
I jump over slopes like a deer.
I fly through the branches now,
a lark lingering
on the wind.

For a Winter Sun

Let your beams shine through empty limbs
and lay shadows on leaf-covered lawns.
Winter sun, strike your glare on places
no summer can touch.
And those trees that stay green in any season,
a memory of color
to this now thin landscape.

As the last red leaves of the plum
droop toward the ground,
their scarcity reminds us
of what is left when all is called
back to the earth and our riches
must be accounted for.

In this winter sun, it's the trunk
and branches that matter.
Leaves are decorations,
distractions left over from spring,
when the new songs
blind the eyes with a day
full of more and longer light.

Fall and winter return us
to the edge of the present time,
to the edge where no foot
can be placed without caution.
No foot
that rides on layers
of leaves drenched and shredded
by new rain.

Yes, sidewalks become slippery.
Wooden stairways steam
in the morning sun.

Collars become useful
to protect the vulnerable neck,
bearing the weight
of a head, tilting backwards to examine
the silver ridges, gray-green lichen,
the living armor of the trunk.

A Poem about Love

There is no list for the forgiven.
They are free now;
All choice and no choice.
Walk and breathe like a woman or man
Home for the first time
After a long journey into the wind.

There is no time limit for the inheritors of grace.
They learn to receive as well as give.
Their song is praise.
Their song is struggle.
For the struggle between breath and time
Is the home of any God.

Remembering

Sometimes it's easy
to distance those you love,
to set down the times when voices merged;
and before long, a gap forms.
These people stand in the background,
on the edge of the horizon.
They are acknowledged, even spoken to
but the roots of love now untouched.
Until that day when without plan or
maneuver, the evening brings you
together, alone with each other.
And you see a person who longs for love,
once special to your life,
and who cared for you.

You go home,
wonder what has happened
all this time, how could I forget
this woman, this man.
Thinking all along you were still friends,
but no life was there,
only easy patterns of fathering and mothering.
But no love,
and worse, no sight.

The Chain

Cut the link loose,
you know, that ring, that circle
you keep rounding.
Cut it loose, let the two ends
dangle into beginning.
Open it up, stretch it out,
make the opening bigger than
the boundary.
A circle is fine if it gives way
to another circle
wider in its reach,
complete with a beginning,
a living, and an end.
An end that reaches out
onto a deeper round—
birth, death, birth, death.
Death, Life.
Do you know where you are
on your circle?
If you don't,
go on home
and sit silently…
then cut the ring loose
and fall,
and fall,
through the opening.

Let Your Colors Run

Sometimes a good home is hard to find
especially inside your body.
Too often we heave and jerk,
constricting ourselves with wire.

When I worry, I know
it's time to cry; even a tear
can burn a man or woman.
Tomorrow my body will weigh more
from the color.

When I grieve too long, I stay
perched on my nerves, my chest
holds a cupped bird.
The day will reach its end,
forcing the serious hand,
sounding out its veins.

I know words can roll
down my chin into your lap.
If I could gather your concerns,
I'd swallow all the blue
that lingers on the morning.
A watercolor is a gathered life.
Let your colors
run down your face.

The Thin Line of Light

Lost in a full moon,
I worry the weary with nonsense
Tossing pennies
Headlong into ponds...
Hoping for arms and mouth
Waiting to hear the sounds
Echo through my ribs.
Music flows in and out of my heart
Pushing the clogs of blood.

Welded to my arteries,
I know the answer lies
Peacefully stowed away
And new,
Receiving the light of apples,
The song of seeds.

I know I am heard
By the thin line of light
Dividing the perils of dying,
And the qualms of birth
Looking over my shoulder,
Never forgetting,
The daisies bouncing like
Children in the fields.

Acknowledgments

First and foremost, I would like to acknowledge my beloved wife, Jane Ferguson Flout, for her encouraging spirit, generous labor, and discerning eye in helping bring this book to fruition.

Deep gratitude to Kim Stafford, whose thoughtful and nurturing teaching helped me receive and trust my own voice and rekindle the light and power of poetry within.

Special thanks to Francesca Bell for her kind and ready support.

Many thanks to all the friends and family who listened with love and support: Mickey and Carol Berberian, Dale Biron, Doug and Anna Cook, Susan Davis, Jane Dawson, Kathleen Denison, Lee Doan, Bob and Jane Ellen Ferguson, Norman Flout Jr., Gene McGinnis, Liz Morris, Chris Olson, Elbina Rafizadeh, Stan and Kathryn Scott, Teressa Snyder, Scott Sullender, and Becky Wright.

And thanks to the writing teachers who got me started on the poetry journey: John Savant, Rosalie Moore, and Jean Pumphrey.

And more gratitude than I can speak to the three people who changed my life: Norman Adams, Maria Howard, and Millie Young.

To the editors of the following publications, where three of my poems originally appeared, some in earlier versions: "The Thin Line of Light," and "Let Your Colors Run," in the *Blue Unicorn*; and "Remembering," in the *Suisun Valley Review.*

Finally, my great appreciation to Nola Burger, who designed this book with simplicity and the inviting beauty of nature in mind.

Richard Flout's poetry has appeared in the *Blue Unicorn* and the *Suisun Valley Review*. A practicing psychotherapist, his writing is informed by a wide range of life experiences as a landscape gardener, an Aikido practitioner, a film / improv theater actor, and a singer. He has had a lifelong interest in the arts as they relate to personal growth, as well as integrating one's spirituality with the healing process, and has facilitated contemplative prayer and meditation groups for many years. He and his wife, Jane Ferguson Flout, writer and former journalist, live in San Rafael, California.

www.ingramcontent.com/pod-product-compliance
Lightning Source LLC
Chambersburg PA
CBHW062221150726
47991CB00006B/2371